USE OF THE LONG BOW WITH THE PIKE

originally titled thus:

CONSIDERATIONS OF THE REASONS THAT EXIST FOR REVIVING THE USE OF THE LONG BOW WITH THE PIKE IN AID OF THE MEASURES BROUGHT FORWARD BY HIS MAJESTY'S MINISTERS FOR THE DEFENCE OF THE COUNTRY

by Richard Oswald Mason

Reproduced in Facsimile

With an Introduction by Stephen V. Grancsay

GEORGE SHUMWAY, Publisher

York • Pennsylvania

GEORGE SHUMWAY, *Publisher*

R. D. 7   York   Pennsylvania   17402

INTRODUCTION

The last advocate for the use of the bow in war was Richard Oswald Mason, a member of the Toxophilite Society, who wrote and had published in 1798, a book urging that as it was intended to have a general arming of the people, and probably many of them would from necessity be armed only with pikes, it was advisable they should also have bows. The title is PRO ARIS ET FOCIS — CONSIDERATIONS OF THE REASONS THAT EXIST FOR REVIVING THE USE OF THE LONG BOW WITH THE PIKE IN AID OF THE MEASURES BROUGHT FORWARD BY HIS MAJESTY'S MINISTERS FOR THE DEFENCE OF THE COUNTRY. The frontispiece represents a British Archer and six woodcuts show various positions; in the text are the words of command for each, together with information on the occasions when the position would be taken. We should also note that the author recommends that his bowman-pikeman wears a helmet and a musket-proof breastplate.

In 1625 an effort was made to combine the bow and pike when William Neade published a book entitled THE DOUBLE-ARMED MAN. Neade pointed out that the chief advantage of his combination of bow and pike was that pikemen, by using their bows, would be enabled to take part in the preliminary actions of a battle, instead of being observers only. Mason's plan is apparently borrowed from Neade's THE DOUBLE-ARMED MAN, though he does not refer to this book.[1] He was also apparently influenced by the revival of interest in archery caused by the activities of the members of the Toxophilite Society which was founded in 1781.

Mason's book, which is reproduced here after a copy in the writer's library, was published primarily to alert the English people to the necessity of being properly armed to protect the country which was in danger of attack by Napoleon. In October 1797 the Directory appointed General Bonaparte to command the army designated to invade England. On 23 February 1798 Bonaparte recommended to postpone the invasion until the French could gain naval supremacy. Napoleon's great Army of Invasion was encamped on the heights above Boulogne in the years about

---

1. William Neade. THE DOUBLE-ARMED MAN. Printed for I. Grismand, at the signe of the Gun in Pauls Alley, London, 1625.
   Neade's book has been published in facsimile by George Shumway Publisher, York, Pennsylvania, 1970.

1800. The English forces were supplemented by a great new force of volunteers that sprang up everywhere, and remained in being until 1814.

From 1595, when the longbow was officially withdrawn as standard military equipment, the writings in favor of its use in warfare were patriotic. We should recall that in recommending the revival of the longbow and pike that the contemporary military firearms were not very efficient. The flintlock musket (a muzzle-loading smooth-bore gun) and common black powder remained the principal destructive agents until well after the Napoleonic wars.

In 1801 a notice to the inhabitants of districts through which the French army might perhaps advance in the course of its projected invasion reminds them that where people are dispersed and act individually "any degree of precision with a common musquet is not to be reckoned on at a greater distance than from fifty to sixty paces." This was, indeed, a hopeful estimate. Colonel Lord Cottesloe, an authority, noted in his book THE ENGLISHMAN AND THE RIFLE, that in 1844, in training with the musket, the first target for recruits was circular and 8 feet in diameter, and the shooting began at 30 yards; they then proceeded to 50, 80, and 100 yards, using the same target. There was even firing for the trained man at 200 yards. It was literally true, however, Colonel Cottesloe continues, that the musket could not be depended on to hit a haystack at that distance, and the conclusion drawn by one observer from some trials in the middle of the last century, just before the rifle superseded it, was that one man might sit in a shair and be shot at all day by another 500 yards away without danger, provided only the firer would aim every shot at him! It has often been said that the effect of the military musket was limited to the wasting of gunpowder and in making a noise.

Nevertheless, T. Roberts in THE ENGLISH BOWMAN, published in 1801, pointed out that the bullet has the decided advantage of the arrow, in three very important particulars, namely: velocity, force, and point blank range. By means of the first, it reaches its object (supposing it to be distant one hundred yards) in less than the fourth part of a second of time, while an arrow (from one of the strongest bows) does not move that space in less than three seconds. As to force, the arrow beyond two hundred and fifty or two hundred and eighty yards at the furthest, does not possess a force equal to what a bullet retains at that distance. But the chief advantage of the musket lies in the extent of its point-blank range, which is calculated to be about one hundred and twenty yards; whereas the strongest bow cannot command a point-blank range much exceeding fifty yards.

Wellington grasped the limitations of the musket of his day, that it was a deadly weapon at point-blank range, but nearly useless at a distance. In the sixteenth century, the bowman was provided with 24 arrows. Of the 24 arrows 8 should be lighter than the residue, to gall the enemy with the hailshot of light arrows, before the bullets can touch the archers.

The pike, like the bow, has been used in warfare throughout history. While the bow had been used only on infrequent occasions in European warfare after the late sixteenth century, the pike continued in use both in the army and navy. After the French Revolution, the pike was used extensively in France, since weapons of any kind were scarce. For example, I have before me a printed pamphlet published in 1792 of a decree authorizing the use of iron grilles confiscated from suppressed religious houses for the manufacture of pikes. During the Spanish War of Independence (1808-1809), the Spaniards routed the troops of Napoleon with pikes. Mason apparently was willing to use the English pike against the French pike, but rapid changes were also being made in other weapons, especially the French mobile artillery. The French artillery was the best in Europe, for though the father of modern gunnery was an Englishman, Benjamin Robins, the greatest progress in artillery was made in France under the direction of Gribeauval. In the battles of this period. because of the short effective range of the musket, horse artillery could gallop within 350 yards of an enemy and batter his battalions.

A great variety of combination weapons have been made during the centuries. Firearms were added to maces, swords, boar spears, etc. The linstock consisted of a pike with the addition of lateral branches on each side of the head that were intended to hold the match for firing cannon. Before the linstock was introduced in the sixteenth century, the cannonier had to discard his pike in order to apply the match to the touch-hole, and was frequently slain in the process. The linstock ensured that he remained armed. The musket readily lent itself to the double application of a projectile weapon and a bayonet.

Much of Mason's book is devoted to a discourse on the success of the bow in past times. The author cites numerous historical instances of the power of the bow in warfare. He repeated the same appeal on behalf of the bow as a weapon of war that had so often been presented by previous writers. We are reminded that Mason's plan was to revive the use of the bow and pike for home defense. The time was obviously badly chosen for such a reversal, to use obsolete types of weapons when Napoleon was so successful with new methods and equipment. Napoleon's invasion plans were cancelled, but we may be certain that the English had been prepared to meet him with the same kind of weapons that were used at Waterloo.

In a few years after the publication of Mason's book, military firearms took a long leap from medieval features to modern. The Baker British military rifle (a flintlock muzzle-loader) was introduced in 1800. This was the first firearm used by the British that could be depended upon to hit a man at 100 yards. When the Rifle Brigade was re-armed in 1838 with the Brunswick rifle, the percussion system was adopted for that rifle and for the troops generally. The detonating system, which substituted a fulminate for flint as a means of igniting the charge of powder, was invented by the Rev. Alexander Forsyth in 1805. Forsyth's invention gave instantaneous discharge and greatly improved the certainty of fire. It ultimately made breech-loading practicable, because each charge when made up, could contain its own ignition. The Snider rifle, designed in 1864, was the first breech loader generally issued to the British Army.

In England during World War II pikes had actually been issued to Home Guard units. These modern pikemen were well aware that the anticipated invaders had machine guns that could fire six hundred shots a minute in a steady stream like water from a hose.

Stephen V. Grancsay
Curator Emeritus of Arms & Armor
Metropolitan Museum of Art
31 January 1970

The BRITISH ARCHER.

"PRO ARIS et FOCIS"

Considerations

of the Reasons that exist for Reviving the use

OF THE

Long Bow with the Pike

IN AID

of the Measures brought forward by

HIS MAJESTY'S MINISTERS

for the

DEFENCE of the COUNTRY

By

Rich.d Oswald Mason Esq.r

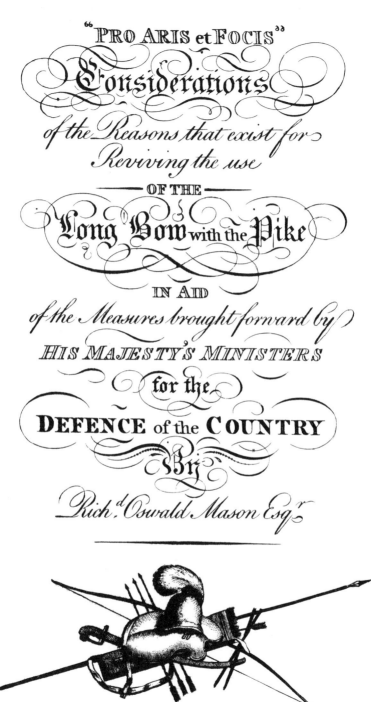

LONDON,

Printed for T. Egerton, Military Library Whitehall.

1798.

Fig. 2.

Fig. 1.

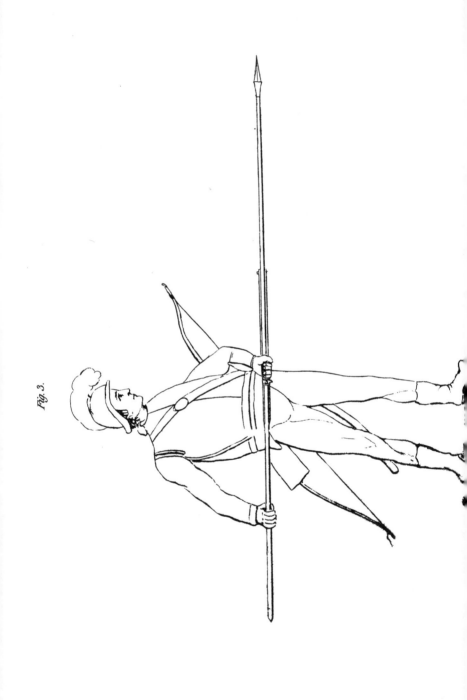

Fig. 3.

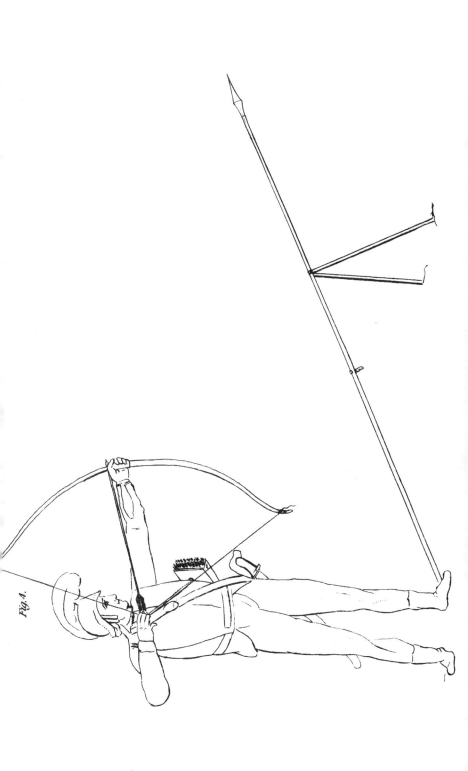

Fig. 4.

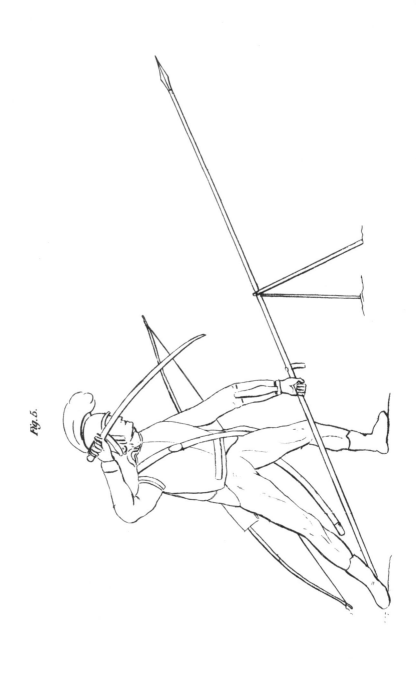

Fig. 5.

Fig 6.

BRITISH PUBLIC.

AT the Voice of the Country in Danger, as it is the Duty of every one to contribute Exertion, when Property, Liberty and National Independence is fo deeply menaced by an afpiring Enemy, I have been induced to bring forward, in this little Treatife, certain Ideas on a Subject, I have long thought might render effential Service. On Reflection of the Caufes which principally gave rife to the overwhelming Military Power of France, which menaced with Subjection every State in Europe, it appeared to me attributable to the Number and Excellence of her Artillery, and to the new Tactics, which Fire Arms facilitate, of bringing forward Superiority of Number with great and certain Advantage; Means which are afforded the French from a great Population,

B which

which the neighbouring Powers do not poſſeſs.
In the Event of this Country having alone to contend with France (although we have now both
Spain and Holland beſide) the Conſequences were
apprehended that the Number and the vaſt natural and acquired Reſources of that State, might
operate in the preſent Mode of War to our infinite
Diſadvantage, from the Neceſſity of withdrawing
a greater Proportion of uſeful Members from Agri-
culture, Manufactures and Commerce, in order
to put us in efficient Power to oppoſe their ordinary Exertion; and that the great attendant Expence, and the conſequent Operation on the Re-
venue, might certainly tend materially to injure
our Finances ; a Situation of Warfare and Exertion, which the Enemy could long maintain by
continual Menaces and Alarms. No Change of
Rulers or Form of Government, it was rationally
ſuppoſed, could ever alter the hoſtile Views of
France againſt this Country, as being founded in
rival Intereſt, and Peace in this Caſe as alone to
be ſecured by being always prepared for War.
That whatever Government might ſucceed the

preſent

present in that Country, we should not have less Cause for Preparation. The Monarchy would be necessarily possessed of all the great Acquisitions made by the Republic; and without Doubt, the Rivalry and Jealousy of France as to this Country is not confined to any Form of Government, as our History well evinces; the Walls of the Court would as well resound with " Delenda est Carthago," as those of the Republican Councils. As these simple Considerations led to the Conclusion, that France and her Allies would naturally ever retain their Interests to abase this Country, so it imperiously required that Britain should oppose with united Exertion, and the Spirit of her ancient Glory. It appeared on Reflection of the Means of maintaining such long continued Exertion, that from the comparative Strength and Resources of the contending Nations, that we ought to be able to effect this with great Inferiority of Number in the Field, so as not to be exhausted by disproportionate Exertion. Though the Power and Excellence of our Ordnance is certainly great,

though

though the natural Superiority of our Cavalry is indisputable yet Advantage of Number will even in these Respects greatly operate. But particularly in the present Mode of War there appeared no Means of supplying great Deficiency in point of Number of Infantry (to which the Enemy owes his greatest Advantages, and on which he placed his reliance) when the Troops on both Sides are equally disciplined, inured to fire, and well commanded. This occasioned the Conclusion, that it was the Nature of the Arms used that prevented our obtaining Advantages with Inferiority of Number as in former Times. On entering into the Examination of the Merits of our ancient Weapons which gave us that Superiority, it appeared on Comparison with the Effect of Small Arms, that the Use of the Long Bow in the Field has been disused without due Consideration, and more from Prejudice, though evidently the only Weapon that can always afford Advantage even to great Inferiority, from its Excellence depending on greater Powers of Strength, Activity and calm Resolution, than any other Nation possesses equal to the British

(and

(and particularly the Englifh.) The reviving the Ufe of Archery together with the Pike, prefented, therefore, in every Point of View the greateft Utility from its Effect in the prefent Time, either to oppofe Cavalry or Infantry, the Confideration of which is offered in the following Lines, together with the general Defcription of the Manual Exercife of the two Weapons when united. As in the prefent intended general Arming of the People, the far greater Mafs may from Neceffity be armed with the Pike, under every Reafon it is evident, the Ufe of the Bow fhould be added to it; for inde-pendant of its fuperior Effect, it is the only efficient Weapon of reach, that can conveniently be ufed with the Pike without being cumberfome to the Individual; without miffile Weapons it will be impoffible to act with Annoyance to the Enemy, but great Lofs muft be fuftained in moft Situations, without Power of Offence. But the Ufe of the Bow being added, will produce fuch Effects as to excite a wonder it has been fo long neglected, and ftrike the Enemy with Amaze, and Terror even of vaft Inferiority. The reviving in this Manner

B 3 the

the Ufe of Archery is ftrongly recommended to the Britifh Youth, to all who are fenfible not to have degenerated from the Force and Spirit of their Anceftors, and who recall to Mind with National Pride and Emulation the Exploits at-chieved by the Valiant Englifh Bowmen. The Enemy will by its Effect foon find, that we are ftill the fame as at Creffy, Poitiers and Agincourt, and the Fear of renewing this Remembrance on his own Territory may induce an honorable Peace, which if enfuing from this Caufe, he will never venture to interrupt, as long as Britifh Nerves retain their Vigor; it fhould be confidered by thofe who may be induced to arm in this Manner, that they are thereby fo completely appointed as to infpire the greateft Confidence, and the well known Effects which the Bow has produced, may well juftify it in the prefent Time, for any juft Caufes that appear to the contrary. No Advantage can be loft by thus ufing the Bow; and when in the Trial its Powers will appear as ample as I have afferted, how well will the Experiment be juftified which is liable to fuch important Confequences.

Should

Should in this Center of the Kingdom be found 1000 Individuals, Nobles, Gentry and Citizens, who may fo bring forward their Service, they will foon perceive its Aavantages, and incite the more general Extenfion of the Meafure, from the Force of fuch refpectable Example.

CONSIDERATIONS, &c.

WHEN the Utility of the Revival of Archery is urged, a fuperficial Idea of the Powers of the Bow may raife a Smile in many, from little Eftimation of its Effect, which has only been feen in a defultory Manner in thefe Times as an Amufement; and from the Prejudice imbibed in Favor of Fire-Arms. But it fhould be regarded with fome Opinion of its Power, as the Caufe of the famous Victories of our Edwards and Henries,

> The firft who deep impreffed on haughty Gaul
> The Terror of thy Arms
> That awes her Genius ftill.
>
> THOMSON.

In ancient Times the greateft Conquefts and Victories were atchieved by the Bow, it enabled the lefs numerous, though more ftrong and active

People,

People, to withstand the mightiest Empires; the Scythian Tribes were held as Invincible, even against the Persian Hosts, though themselves were Bowmen; the Romans in their Height of Power and Dominion, though Conquerors of Europe, Africa, and the East, could yet make no Impression on the Monarchy of the Arsacides, but were for Ages defeated in all their Attempts by the Parthian Archers. The Alans, Huns, and Dacii, who finally overthrew the Empire of the West, were remarkable for Archery. It was by Means of the Bow, that the Arabian Tribes, emerging from their confined and desert Territory, established the vast Power of the Caliphs. After them, the Turks, by the same Weapon, overthrew the Eastern Empire, bereft the European Powers of some of their finest Provinces, menaced Christendom, and preserved a formidable State so long as they retained its Use in full Vigour. These Nations, and all others who have excelled in Archery, were distinguished for Activity and Strength, kept up and inured by Practice and Martial Exercises: Since those Days, the only Nation who has excelled in

the

the Power of ufing the Bow, has been the Englifh, the Exploits of whofe Archers has equalled, if not furpaffed, whatever is recounted of thofe of the former Nations. For after their adopting its Ufe, fubfequent to the Norman Conqueft, they fo greatly improved its Power over all other Nations, owing to fuperior perfonal Strength, and to that cool and fteady tempered Refolution, which is ab-folutely effential to excel in Archery,* as to render all other of their Contemporaries (even the Nor-mans themfelves afterwards, who had introduced it) unable to oppofe them with any chance of Succefs, which occafioned them to refort to every Invention to withftand its Effect, either by the unwieldy Crofs-Bow, or the ftrongeft Armour, which ob-tained fo much with the French, even after the Difufe of the Bow, as to be a great Incum-

---

* This Temper of Mind which is peculiar to the Englifh in Action, gave them great Advantage ; the Impetuofity of the French Character was, and ftill is, an infuperable Ob-ftacle to their Excellence in the Ufe of the Bow, though it acts in their Favor with the Mufket. As to the Neceffity of calm Refolution in the Archer, vide ASCHAM, Book II. Page 228.

brance

brance to them*, yet in no wife preventing the Effect of the Shot of the Englifh Archers †, who
were more dreaded than any other Troops in the
World ‡, continually gaining the moft decifive

* Vide Montaigne's Effays, Vol. II.

† Befides what muft appear evident from their great Vic-
tories in France, gained over Adverfaries in the ftrongeft
Armour, I fhall quote an Inftance of their Power from
Walfingham the Hiftorian, defcribing their Effect at the
Battle of Holmedon Hill, againft the Scots, in the Time of
Henry IV. " Thus the Glory of the Victory was entirely
" owing to the Archers, who delivered their Arrows fo
" brifkly, fo warmly, and fo effectually, that they battered
" the Helmets, they fplit the Swords, they fhivered the
" Lances, and the beft tempered Mail proved but a weak
" Defence againft the Execution they did."

GUTHRIE's *Hiftory of England*, Vol. II.

‡ Montluc, in his Commentaries, fpeaking of the Siege
of Calais, at which he was prefent, ftates, that it was a tradi-
tional faying in his Time in France, " that one Englifhman
" would beat three Frenchmen, and that the Englifh
" would never fly nor never yield ;" which had no doubt
been derived from Experience. The fame Teftimony was
given by the Breton Generals to the Englifh, before the
Battle of St. Aubin, in the Time of Henry VII. when they
ordered 1200 of their Troops to carry the red Crofs, for
to imprefs the French with the Dread of their being Englifh.
The fame Impreffion feized the French at the Battle of the
Spurs, in the Time of Henry VIII.

Victories,

Victories, with great Difparity of Number, over every Nation with whom they contended in Arms : and it is worthy of Remark, that as being excellent Archers, gave feveral of the Nations before mentioned, the Power of refifting, nay conquering more numerous, and otherwife more powerful Nations ; fo alfo it in like Manner acted in Favour of the Englifh, who, with Scotland againft them, (then being the intimate Ally of France) Ireland of no Affiftance, but rather held as a dependant Conqueft, yet did they ten feveral Times fuccefsfully invade France *, once brought it to the Brink of Ruin †, once conquered it ‡, made one of its Monarchs Prifoner §, and another tributary ‖. The Source of Detraction and Lofs of this amazing

* In 1339, 1346, 1355, 1359, 1415, 1417, 1421, 1475, 1513, 1544.

† France was brought to all but abfolute Conqueft by Edward III.

‡ Under Henry V.

§ King John made Prifoner at the Battle of Poitiers, with his Son Philip and moft of his Nobility.

‖ Lewis XI. who fubmitted to pay a Tribute to Edward IV. to relieve himfelf from the Terror of Englifh Arms.

Glory

Glory, was our Civil Diffentions, which afforded to the Enemy the Means of regaining thofe Advantages with Eafe, which had been obtained with Difficulty. A memorable Leffon, inftructing us, that the Glory and Power which is atchieved by the united Will and Force of a Nation can alone be maintained by equal Exertions. The fatal Spirit of Party, which in the Reign of Henry VI. infected the Court, Camp and City, contributed more to the Lofs of our Honor and Conquefts, than the Enemy's Arms. Similar Caufes in all Times produce like Effects, and the Rife and Decadence of States are caufed either by the Force of Union and Energy, or Effects of a contrary Principle. It is an Affertion I am of Opinion may be well maintained, feeing the great Authorities that exift in its Support as well from ancient, as modern Hiftory of Nations, that a People, however comparatively inferior in many Refpects, yet, if united, cannot but be invincible,*

* This may be obferved from the Struggle made by the once Great States of Holland againft Philip II. and the juftnefs of their Motto, " Parvæ Res Concordia crefcunt.' as alfo from the Exertions of the ancient Swifs, in defence of their Independence againft the greater Powers of the Time.

and

and it is fincerely hoped, at the prefent eventful
Æra, that mindful as well of the Virtues as the
Faults of our Anceftors, we may, by adopting
their Energy, maintain unfullied the high Repu-
tation and Glory of the Britifh Name. But I return to ftate, that as to the Powers requifite for the
efficient Ufe of the Bow, equal Ability exifts in the
People of this Country as at any former Period,
the prefent Race appears in no wife degenerated
in point of Force of Body, as the flighteft Obfervation on the Stature and Form of the general
Mafs of the People, as well as on the Caufes that
tend to produce or increafe that Strength, will render eafily difcernable ; and it is proved by con-
fidering that by the ancient Statutes, it was required of every Man from 18 to 35 Years to
fhoot in a Bow capable of carrying 11 Score
Yards; in the prefent Time, among thofe who
practife for Amufement, there is fcarce a ftrong
Archer, that cannot fhoot that Diftance at a Flight,
and fome even as far as 15 Score Yards. As our
Powers cannot but be deemed equal to its Ufe, it
is ftated, in order to point out the Advantage of
Archery

Archery in the prefent Times, that in direct re-
verfe of the Effect of the Bow, Fire-Arms brought
the Nations to an Equality, and acted greatly in
favor of the Weakeft, though more numerous, if
equally brave and capable of Difcipline. A Man
of ordinary Strength and irregular Make may be
able to handle the Piece as well as another of
greater Powers, but not equal to manage a ftrong
Bow; from the Time of this Change taking place
in arming the Infantry, it is but in rare Inftances,
that great Inferiority of Number has obtained fuch
Victories as formerly, againft equally difciplined
Troops; † though in moft Actions fince thofe
Times when Number was more balanced, though
yet in favor of the Enemy, the Britifh Superiority
has appeared with diftinguifhed Pre-eminence;
but Succefs with great Difparity is particularly
obviated by the Mode of Tactics lately introduced
by the French, of acting in Columns, and continually

† The Decifion of the Battles of Wynendale and Minden,
and feveral others in modern Times, may be traced to the
particular ill Conduct, or the undifciplined State of the
Enemy.

relieving

relieving with frefh Troops when neceffary, there-by wearing out their Adverfaries more by the Fatigue of long continued Exercife, than the Ef-fect of their Fire; and it muft be admitted from the Events of this War, that thefe Manœuvres have had their Impreffion upon naturally the beft Troops in Europe in obftinate Actions even of Days continuance, though attended with little com-parative Lofs.

Though Fire-Arms give the Advantage to Num-ber, yet the Englifh Archers formerly never regarded it*, not hefitating to attack and van-quifh great Superiority. The Confequences of the total Difufe of the Bow, and the Variablenefs in Changing it entirely without good Reafon, were apprehended by many at the Time. Lord Herbert,

---

* Early in the Morning of the Battle (of Agincourt) Henry fent out a Welch Captain, one David Gam, to reconnoitre the Force and Difpofition of the Enemy. Gam being returned, in Report told His Majefty, that there were of the French enough to fight, enough to be flain, and enough to run away. GUTHRIE's HISTORY, Vol. II. Note in this Battle was flain 10,000; and 14,000 taken Prifoners, by 14,000 Troops in great part enfeebled by Sicknefs.

reafoning

reafoning againſt its Diſuſe, ſtates the Uſe
of the Bow to be in Favor of the Engliſh from
their perſonal Strength, which made up for Inferiority of Number*. The learned Aſcham alſo
in his Treatiſe on Archery ſenſibly deprecates its
Decay, and the Changing the Uſe of the Long-
Bow for any other Weapon, as that to which
the Engliſh were moſt apt and capable, but to be
made an Amuſement of in Peace and a Defence
in War, that it ſhould be joined with the other
Arms for the better Defence of the Realm†. But
many other Teſtimonies are given of its Utility,
even from the Time in which Fire-Arms began
generally to obtain, till a late Period, after its

---

* The Reaſons are ſo pointed that I ſhall give his own
Words: " What though with our 12 or 15,000 we have
" oft defeated their Armies of 50,000 or 60,000, ſtands it
" with Reaſon of War to expect the like Succeſs ſtill ?
" eſpecially ſeeing the Uſe of Arms is changed, and for
" the Bow, proper for Men of our Strength, the Caliver
" begins to be generally received."
                    LORD HERBERT's *Life and Reign of Henry* VIII.
                    Page 18. Ed. 1649.

† Vide Aſcham's Toxophilus, Book I. page 12.

                                        total

total Difufe in War,* fome of which, as very ingenious and explanatory, may be feen at full in
the Notes; befides thefe Authorities, many good
Reafons are alledged as to its Utility at the prefent
Time

* " The Law of Archery made before, was not only
" confirmed, but made perpetual; fo that notwithftanding
" the Ufe of Calivers or Hand-Guns, it was thought fit
" to continue the Bow. While he that carries the Caliver
" goes unarmed, the Arrow will have the fame Effect
" within its Diftance as the Bullet, and can for one Shot
" return two. Befides as they ufed their Halberts with
" their Bows, they could fall on the Enemy with great
" Advantage."
    LORD HERBERT's *Life and Reign of Henry* VIII. Page 55.

" As it was certainly by Help of the Broad Arrow and the
" Long-Bow, that the Normans conquered England, fo
" was it by the fame Weapon, that the Englifh afterwards
" conquered France; I fhall therefore here give the Reader
" an excellent and curious Comparifon between this Wea-
" pon and our Fire-Arms, as I find it in the Life of William
" by J. H.—One Circumftance more I hold fit to be
" obferved, that this Victory was gotten only by Means of
" the Blow of an Arrow, the Ufe whereof was brought
" into this Land. Afterwards the Englifh being trained
" to that Fight, did thereby chiefly maintain themfelves
" with honourable Advantage againft all Nations with
" whom they did contend in Arms, being generally reputed
" the beft Shot in the World. But of late Years it has
" been altogether laid afide, and inftead thereof the Har-

quebuz

Time by the learned and judicious **Mr. Grofe,**
who clearly points out its great Effect, either
againft Cavalry or Infantry, and the Power the
Archers

" quebuz and Caliver are brought into Ufe, yet not
" without Contradiction of many expert Men of Arms, who
" albeit they do not reject the Ufe of the fmall Pieces, yet
" do they prefer the Bow before them. Firft, for that in
" a reafonable Diftance, it is of greater both Certainty
" and Force. Secondly, for that it difcharges fafter. Thirdly,
" for that more Men may difcharge therewith at once;
" for only the front Ranks difcharge with the Piece,
" neither hurt they any but thofe that are in Front; but
" with the Bow ten or twelve Ranks may difcharge toge-
" ther and will annoy as many Ranks of the Enemy.
" Laftly, for that an Arrow doth ftrike more Parts of the
" Body, for in that it hurteth by Defcent and not only
" point blank like the Bullet, there is no Part of the Body,
" but it may ftrike, from the Crown of the Head even to
" the nailing the Foot to the Ground; hereupon it fol-
" loweth, that the Arrows falling fo thick as Hail on the
" Bodies of Men, as lefs fearful of their Flefh, fo more
" flenderly armed than in former times, muft neceffarily
" produce moft dangerous Effects. Befides thefe general
" Refpects, in many particular Services and Times the
" Ufe of the Bow is of great Advantage. If fome Defence
" lie before the Enemy, the Arrow may ftrike when
" the Bullet cannot; foul Weather may much hinder the
" Difcharge of the Piece, but it is of no great Impediment
" to the Shot of the Bow. A Horfe ftruck with the Bullet,

if

Archers have of acting in Situations, where other Troops cannot *. The Reasons given, shew the Causes why the English Archers were enabled to gain

" if the Wound be not mortal, may perform good Service, " but if an Arrow is faſtened in his Fleſh, the continual " Stirring thereof, occaſioned by the Motion of himſelf, " will force him to caſt off all Command, and either bear " down or diſorder thoſe that are near. But the Crack " of the Piece, ſome Men ſay, doth ſtrike a Terror into " the Enemy: True, if they be ſuch as never heard the " like Noiſe before; but a little Uſe will extinguiſh theſe " Terrors to Men; yea, to Beaſts, acquainted with theſe " Cracks, they work a weak Impreſſion of Fear: and if it " be true, as all Men of Action do hold, that the Eye in " all Battles is firſt overcome, then againſt Men equally ac- " cuſtomed to both, the Sight of the Arrow is more avail- " able to Victory than the Crack of the Piece. "

GUTHRIE's *Hiſtory of England*, Vol. I. Page 323, a Note.

* " The Long-Bow might, on ſome Occaſions, undoubt- " edly at this Time, be uſed with great Advantage, particu- " larly againſt Cavalry; a few Horſes, wounded by Arrows " left ſticking in them, would probably become ſo unruly as " to diſorder a whole Squadron. Beſides, the Sight and " Whizzing of the Arrows before the Heads of thoſe " Horſes they did not hit, would keep them in a conſtant " State of Terror and Reſtiveneſs; nor would a Flight of " Arrows, falling on a Battalion of Foot, fail of a conſider- " able Effect, independent of the Men they killed or " wounded, as when ſhot with an Elevation, they would " be viſible almoſt from the Time they left the Bow, and

" it

gain fuch Advantages over the Men at Arms as
to drive them by their barbed Arrows, either off
the Field or upon their own Foot. But, on the
Change to Fire Arms, the Cavalry was rendered
fuperior to the Infantry, from their Difcharge not
being fo galling, or of equal Dread, fo that the
Horfe have generally been able, fince thofe Days,
to bear down the Infantry by the Weight of their
Charge, as the Accounts of moft Actions in modern Times exemplifies : By the Change we therefore loft a great Advantage, for before it our Cavalry and Infantry were both fuperior to all Pur-
pofes.

The Caufes to which are attributed the Difufe
of the Bow, are fuppofed to arife from the Power
and Effect of Fire-Arms being little known on

" it would require a more than ordinary Exertion of Cou-
" rage to refrain from looking at them, and endeavouring
" by fome Movement to avoid them ; this, by engroffing
" the Attention of the Men, would prevent their acting
" with Vigour againft a Batalion oppofed to them. Archers
" could act in the Rear of a Battalion of Infantry, and
" even of a Squadron of Cavalry."
GROSE, *Hiftory of the Englifh Army*, Vol. I. Page 148, a Note.

their

their firft Introduction, but conceived of more, than they really poffeffed, an Opinion which heightened by the Fire and Noife attending their Difcharge, induced the Archers to diftruft their Bows, from efteeming them of not fufficient Reach, as to put them on an Equality with thofe Arms of a greater Power of Range, and in Confequence the Change took place, in order to give Confidence. But certainly could our Anceftors have witneffed the fruitlefs long continued Firing of Mufketry (after its being brought to its higheft Improvement) in the Actions of Hours, even Days in modern War, with the little comparative Lofs, to what was fuftained when Archery was ufed, * they would have not been

fo

* Refpecting the great Inefficiency attending the Firing of Mufketry in modern War, and the confequent Expence attending it, it may be judged of by what is ftated by Marfhal Count Saxe, in his Memoirs, that, on a Computation of the Balls ufed in a Day's Action, not one of upwards of Eighty-five took place.

By the Obfervation on Battles of a later Date, its Effect falls infinitely fhort of the above Proportion, which can be clearly proved by the Review of the various Actions of the

C 4 prefent

fo readily, from Prejudice, out of conceit with their famous Weapon, but it would have remained in Eftimation to the prefent Time. It was rarely neceffary for the Archers to empty their Quivers

to

prefent Continental War. As a fufficient Inftance to govern the Reft, I fhall cite its Effect at the Battle before Tournay, the 22d May, 1794, between the French and the Allies, an Action the moft obftinately difputed on both Sides, from fix A. M. till nine at Night, the French lofing at the higheft Calculation, 10,000 men, killed and wounded, the Allies 5.000 ; the Country oppofing little Interruption from the Nature of the Ground, being entirely plain and no Cover, but flight Hedges or the Grain then ftanding. The French brought into Action 100,000 Men, the Allies 60,000, reckoning the Proportion of our Infantry at 40,000, and fuppofing, at a moderate Average, that this Body of Men at leaft expended 32 Rounds each Man, all Circumftances confidered, form a Total of 1,280,000 Balls difcharged, to occafion the above Lofs of the Enemy, making 128 Shots. to the difabling one Object, without bringing into Computation the Proportion of the Lof. that might have been occafioned by the Bayonet, the Cavalry and Artillery, though thefe Caufes that Day may be reafonably concluded to have occafioned half the Lofs, and in this Cafe upwards of 236 Shots of Mufketry muft have been ufed to difable one Man. The fame Deduction may be drawn from a more general Review of all the Actions in modern War ; but at the Diftance at which Mufketry can act with any Effect, as far as nine Score Yards,

it

to obtain the moſt memorable Victories, a few Diſcharges, well directed, were ſufficient to break the beſt Troops, and that in Times when the ſtrongeſt Armour was worn to prevent their Effect. At Agincourt one Diſcharge of the Archers, under the Duke of York, overthrew 2400 Men at Arms, at the Onſet of the Battle. So conquering a Weapon was the Bow, that the Enemy could ſcarcely either fight or fly, ſo that beſide the Carnage, the Engliſh have taken Priſoners, as at Poitiers, double the Number of their whole Army. In theſe Times, the continued Roar and menacing Danger of Cannon and Muſketry, preſents to the Soldier nothing but the Idea of preſent Death; although he is afterwards ſurpriſed at the Loſs being ſo comparatively ſmall to what Imagination had

---

it is aſſerted that in the Diſcharge of a Body of well trained Archers, allowing even great Deficiency, at leaſt one Shaft in Ten would hit, ſo as to kill or wound an Object. Here then evidently appears an Advantage in Favor of the Bow, in point of Certainty of its Shot, of no leſs than upwards of Twenty to One ! ! ! And as the Archer has the Power of diſcharging two Shots at leaſt for one of his Adverſary, the above Proportion is even doubled.

heightened

heightened the Danger. But notwithſtanding this apparent Terror of the modern Arms, yet there never has exiſted real Cauſe for the Archer to diſtruſt his Bow againſt ſmall Arms; on the contrary, the reverſe is evident from Reaſon and Demonſtration. In the preſent Time, the Revival of its Uſe muſt be attended with the greateſt Succeſs and Advantage; as it cannot but be admitted we poſſeſs equal Powers to its efficient Uſe from our perſonal Strength and Activity. I ſhall therefore deſcribe the Arming of the Archer, which muſt certainly appear to carry great Superiority and Efficiency.

The Archer completely armed, carries his LongBow and Quiver of twenty-four Sheaf-Arrows, the Bow proportioned to his Strength and proved in its Power and Elaſticity*. Theſe, when not uſing them, are ſlung at his Back: he is alſo provided with a Pike about ten Feet in length, which, when in Action, and uſing his Bow, he ſtrikes beſide

---

* The aſcertaining the Power of the Bow and proving its Elaſticity by weighing it, is the Invention of the ingenious Mr. Thomas Waring.

him,

him, or grounds through the Files ; and when neceffary to prevent the Breaking in of Cavalry, he plants in Front ; it is fupported by two Spikes which fall from the Staff of the Pike, and when extended, fupport it prefented, as high as the Breaft of a Horfe, or Middle of a Man.* Two files of the Archers thus plant their Pikes, when fo attacked, and as they oppofe a Defence not to be broke in upon, they can at the fame Time pour fo dreadful and offenfive a Shower of Arrows, as to deftroy, wound and throw into Diforder any Affailants. When acting on the Offenfive, they advance under continual well directed Flights at Intervals, and then charge with their Spears, if neceffary, which, being feveral Feet longer than the Mufket and Bayonet, though not fo heavy and unwieldy, are far more formidable. The Archer alfo carries a Broad Sword for clofe Action. Though fo well armed, yet none of his Weapons are in the way of the other. In point of Defence,

---

* The Model of the Pike thus fupported in Defence, may be feen at Mr. Thomas Waring's Manufactory, Charlotte Street, Bloomfbury.

if

if neceffary, without any Inconvenience, he wears
a Breaft-Plate Mufket proof, fimilar to the prefent
Auftrian Cuiraffiers (the Archers always were
fo equipped formerly,) but in all Cafes, he fhould
wear the Helmet, as a more convenient and fecure
Covering for the Head. Thefe are the Outlines
of the complete armed Archer; and the Advantage
of his Service will be herein after pointed out,
if any Thing can be wanting to the Ideas fug-
gefted in the Authorities before cited. The
Practice of his Exercife is maintained at lefs
Expence than any other, the Shot being always
recoverable, and from the Nature of it, he is
rendered a Markfman from the Training of
continual Shooting with Aim, and judging of
Diftance by Shooting at the Butt and Roving,*
which

---

* It is a great Advantage which the Archer poffeffes,
from the Nature of his Weapon, that he has it always in
his Power to judge of his Difcharge by his Arrow lighting
and being able to recover it, from which he can amend
his Shot, by knowing the Caufes, which may deviate its
Direction, and by afcertaining the Powers of his Bow,
give the neceffary Elevation; but this is more difficult
with

which is by no Means fo general with any other
kind of Troops, to whom more Attention is paid
to their Evolutions in Bodies, than to their Individual Skill. As Archers are foon capable of
learning the Acting in Line and Column, their
being Mafters of the Power of their Weapon,
muft neceffarily appear to give them great Advantage. I fhall here defcribe certain of thofe, which
on the cleareft Grounds fhew the Superiority the
Bow would obtain over the Small-Arms of the
Enemy. The Effect of a Mufket Ball cannot be
judged of according to its great Extent of Range,
if fhot in Elevation, which may be 800 Yards
or more, for it cannot for many Reafons be exactly
determined; but from its efficient Direction within
a reafonable Diftance; which, as the Piece is
levelled, is reduced at the higheft Eftimation to

with Fire-Arms; in Shooting at the Target, if the Mark
is miffed, it is impoffible fo precifely to afcertain the Caufe
as with the former. Even in Action, which is of more Im-
portance, the Archer by feeing the Flight of his Arrow can
determine whether it reaches its due Deftination, and
directs his following Shots accordingly.

Note of the Author.

200 Yards,

200 Yards; and the Aim at this Diftance is even very uncertain, from as well the exceeding Diminution of the Objects in the Perfpective as the imperceptible Inequalities of Ground, which Caufes may render the Level either difficult to adjuft, or if correct, defeats it. Little Effect has been done in modern War at this Diftance by the Mufket, and more often the Event is decided by the Bayonet, (of which the Enemy vaunt fo much) after a long Continuance of Firing, which certainly does not advance the Excellence of the Mufket. The Range of a Bow, when difcharged in Elevation, is from 9 to 12 Score Yards, fometimes more, but from the greater Preffure of Air on the Shaft than on the Bullet, and from the Gravity being in the Pile, it defcends at its ultimate Diftance, before it has loft its Force, and will then do good Execution; whereas the Force of a Ball in a like Situation is fpent. A Bullet, if it miffes its Direction, by overfhooting the Object at any Diftance, goes to the utmoft Range without further Effect: the Arrow, if it miffes the Front Ranks, may yet defcend on the Rear, and do equal Execution. At the

the Diftance at which fmall Arms are efficient, the Bow is of more Effect and greater Quicknefs of Exercife.

No Miffile can be fo deftructive and annoying, as the barbed or fheaf Arrow ufed by the Englifh Archers: for if the Object, Man or Horfe, is wounded, he is put out of Action till extracted ; the latter particularly, though ftruck by a Ball, while warm, may continue to act; but the continually galling of an Arrow would certainly render him raging with his Pain, and diforder thofe around him. The Force which is capable of being given to the Arrow, is certainly greatly fuperior to the leaden Bullet, refulting from its Length, its Pile of tempered Iron and pointed Form, calculated for piercing, which may be judged of, by the Archers in former Times having acted againft Adverfaries in the ftrongeft Armour, whereas in thefe Times, the Auftrian Horfe Cuiraffiers carry Breaft-Plates of not above 7lb. Weight, which are mufket-proof.* Let not Prejudice

* The Force with which an Arrow ftruck an Object at a moderate Diftance, may be conceived from an Inftance given

judice fo far interpofe, as to efteem the barbed Arrow a cruel, though certainly it is a deathful Weapon, and at the fame Time pafs over unheeded the Confideration of the more cruel Mutilation of Individuals by the Artillery of modern Times. The Arrow is the ancient Weapon of the Realm, and the reviving its Ufe in Defence of our Rights is but exerting it in the Caufe of Humanity. In point of quick fhooting, from the fimple Exercife of the Bow, there are only the Motions of nocking the Shaft, and drawing up the Bow, which are foon effected with order, fo that an Archer, expertly trained, can fhoot 12 times in a Minute, and a flower from 6 to 8 times. But the Exercife of the Mufket is compofed of more Motions in order to ufe it, which take at leaft twice the Time, however effected, fo that Archers

given by Edward VI. in his Journal, wherein he fays, that an hundred Archers of his Guard fhot before him two Arrows each, and afterwards all together, that they fhot at an Inch Board which fome pierced through and fluck into the other Board; divers pierced it quite through with the Heads of their Arrows: the Board being well feafoned Timber. The Diftance from the Mark is not mentioned.

could

could always be able to return at leaft two fhot for one of the Enemy; the Advantage muft be evident attending the quick Difcharges of fuch galling Showers of Arrows, the Danger of which is feen and apprehended ; is it poffible to fuppofe, but that the greateft Carnage and Confufion muft take place, even with the beft difciplined Troops ? Let an Idea be formed of the Terror of the Object, in fuppofing a Body of a thoufand Archers oppofed to a like Number, or even to great Superiority within their Diftance ; what Impreffion muft it not have on the Enemy, the Sight and Effect of at leaft 6000 Arrows flying upon their Line in a Minute ! under fuch Flights, kept up without In-termiffion, how would it be poffible for them, either Horfe or Foot, to perform their Evolutions or Ex-ercife ; or not fall into Rout and Diforder amidft fuch Carnage and vifible Danger? for Mufketeers are enabled to keep their Order as oppofed to each other, from not feeing it. But under fuch galling Difcharges, if the Cavalry could poffibly pufh to the Charge of the Archers, they then

D   would

would plant their Pikes.* This **Pallifade of a** double Row of Lances would effectually fecure the Ranks of the Archers from being broke,

* The great Ufe and Effect of the Pike, in withftanding Cavalry, may be judged of by the Reafons given in a Military Treatife publifhed in 1589, from the French of Mr. Wm. de Bellay, who writes in Page 26—" But let us pafs further " to fpeak of the Pike, of which although the Switzers " have not been the Inventors, yet have they at the leaft " brought it again into Ufe ; for that they being poore, and " defirous to live at libertie, were conftrained to fight " againft the Princes of Germany, who being rich and of " great Power, did maintain many Horfemen, which the " Switzers could not do, and therefore making thefe " Warres a-foote, they were conftrained to run into the " ancient Manner, and out of it to choofe fome Armes, " wherewith they might defend themfelves againft the " Enemy's Horfemen, which Neceffity had made them ei- " ther to maintain or find out again the Orders of Time " paft, without which Pikes, Foot-Men are wholly unpro- " fitable; they took therefore Pikes, as Weapons not only " fit to withftand Horfemen, but alfo to vanquifh them; " by the Help of which Weapon, and through the Truft " they have in their own good Order, they have taken fuch " a Boldneffe, that fifteen or twenty Thoufand of their " Men dare enterprize upon a whole World of Horfemen, " as they have made proof at Navarre and at Marignan, " although the one Bataille fell out better on their Side, than " the other."

GROSE's *Hiftory of the Englifh Army*, Vol. I. Page 137, a Note.

and

and enable them by their terrible Difcharges to put their Adverfaries to rout. In the Charge of Infantry they would come to the Pufh of Pike, and plainly fhew the Effect of the Spear over the Enemy's Bayonets. With Archers, even a Column of Forty or Fifty deep can difcharge together, and would annoy as many Ranks of the Enemy, if he was advancing in like Order within Bow-Shot, which could not fail, befides the Lofs, of throwing his Column into the greatest Diforder and Confufion, and prevent his acting with any Regularity. The Ufe of the Bow is liable to fewer Impediments than fmall Arms, which may be rendered defective by the Weather, and the various Accidents attending the Lock, the Flint or the Powder; with the Bow, it is only neceffary to be fure of the String, any Number of Difcharges within the Day does not affect it; but the Mufket after long firing grows fo foul as greatly to weaken its Effect. Although the Noife of the Fire may be fuppofed to ftrike Dread and Alarm, yet this Impreffion is eafily removed

by

by Cuſtom; and in that Caſe, among diſciplined Troops, the Sight of the Archers Shot would convey more Terror, than the Noiſe attending the Diſcharge of the Piece. It muſt appear evident to the Judgment of all Military Men, who rightly conſider the acting of Archers, that there are numberleſs Situations of Ground in which they could act with peculiar Effect, not only in the Field, but in the Attack or Defence of Lines they muſt be of the greateſt Service; in the former the Intrenchments as to them are of no Protection to the Enemy, from their ſhooting in Elevation, which muſt be very galling to his Artillery, which could not ſo readily act with Vigour, if in reach of the Arrows, and this would favour our own Artillery. In defending Intrenchments, they would be of equal Advantage to check the Advance of the Enemy's Columns, by their Power of cloſe diſcharging in that Order, if neceſſary, when they themſelves are protected againſt the Enemy's Muſ-ketry. In the Field, there are many Situations from Inequality of Ground, which are nevertheleſs

imperceptible

imperceptible in the Diftance, and yet totally ob-
viate the Effect of the levelled Piece, but not the
elevated Shot of the Bow. The acting of Archers, from thefe Caufes, could not fail in the
prefent Time to afford great Advantages, and occafion Dread and Impreffion on the Enemy. To
effect the Revival of the Ufe of the Bow with the
Improvements in arming the Archer as fet forth,
it is ftrongly recommended to the Attention of the
feveral Societies of Archers, to incite the carrying
the fame into effect by their Example. By their
reviving its Ufe, as one of the Arts of Peace, they
have teftified their Refpect for what was once the
Defence of the Realm; it is therefore fo far their
Duty to the Country at this Crifis, on the juft
Grounds that exift for influencing it, to bring to
efficient Ufe in War, what cannot but greatly
contribute to the prefent and future Safety of the
Country againft the Foreign Invader.

Of an enlightened Public, not influenced by
Prejudice to neglect what can in any degree con-
cern the National Welfare, the greateft Attention is

D 3   expected

expected with Confidence to a Meafure, which will have the Effect of raifing our Renown, and efficiently promote Exertions in Defence of that Liberty and Independence, which our Fore-fathers maintained with their Lives and Fortunes for fo many Ages.

Of

The MANUAL EXERCISE *of the* BOW *and* PIKE.

THE Standing of the Archer is firſt to be con-
ſidered; he muſt have one Foot Space from
his right and left hand Man more than his Square,
in order for the Action of his Bow, the Ranks ſhould
be about one Pace behind the other ; this is called
the open Order. The cloſe Order is, when he
comes up to charge with the Pike, in which he has
no more than his Square. The Archer for the
Word of Command looks to the Right, the Words
of Order are,

Form your Line. { Either two or three deep, as judged neceſſary.

Stand in open Order.
To right, Dreſs.

D 4   FIRST

FIRST POSITION.

The Archer ordered. Vide Fig. I. and Frontifpiece.

THIS Pofture is the Firft, as being ready for all other Services, the Bow and Quiver being at his Back, and the Pike at reft. It is the firft in which the Archer is thrown when in Line, and that which he is always in on Guard, and in the Motions of Parade.

The Words of Order are:

1ft,
Handle your Pike.

> In this the right Hand is lowered on the Pike, and the Left is brought to handle it even with the Shoulder.

2d,
Advance your Pike.

> This is then brought forward and ftruck in Front, fomething fimilar to poifing the mufket.

Trail

3d,
Trail your Pike.

{ This is by lowering the Pikes with the Point to the Ground. In Line, only the front Rank can do this, for obvious Reasons.

The two first Motions are given as the Salute to an Officer, and that made, on relieving Guard. The Third to be used may be thus distinguished: the lowering the Pike to the Left, as a Royal Salute; when to the Right to Commanding Generals.

SECOND

SECOND POSITION.

The Archer Shooting. Vide Fig. II.

THIS is the firſt Poſture of the Archer's acting on the Offenſive, which he enters into as
ſoon as within reach of the Enemy.

The words of Order are :

1ſt,
Strike or ground your Pike.
{ This is, into the ground, at the right Side; but when it will not admit it, it is grounded to the Left along the Ranks.

2d,
Order your Bows.
{ This is the lowering the Bow with the Quiver, draw-ing it from the Sheath and bracing it.

3d,
Make ready Point.
{ This is nocking the Shaft and preſenting it.

Shoot

4th,
Shoot together.

Or, 1ſt, 2d, &c. Company or Battalion, of the right or left Center, the Number of Yards Diſtance being called by the Score and its Proportions.

The Diſtance is aſcertained by the moſt expert Archers on the Right of the Battalion ; by the Serjeants for Inſtance, acting as Flugelmen, which they determine by Judgment of the Eye aided by the Aſſiſtance derived from the Training.

When the Archers are preſſing on in Attack, the Words of Order are :

Shoulder your Pike—
March—Halt.

The Bow at the ſame Time is ported in the left Hand.

The Orders as in the preceding Page, omitting the 2d.

The moſt effectual Mode of Attack, wherever poſſible for the Archers, is, having ordered their Bows, to advance rapidly to an hundred Yards, and then open on the Enemy with a quick Succeſſion of Diſcharges. Scarce an Arrow would fall in vain at this Diſtance.   THIRD

THIRD POSITION.

The Archer Charging. Vide Fig. III.

THIS is the fecond Pofture in Attack, if, after ufing their Bows, and having thrown the Enemy into Diforder by their Flights of Arrows, it is judged proper to come to the Pufh of Pike.

The Words of Order are:

1ft,
Faften your Bow. } In the manner as feen in the Plate.

2d,
Or, Return your Bow. } This is returning it, together with the Quiver, to the right Shoulder, as feen in the 1ft Pofition.

3d, *Recover your Pike.*

* It is to be obferved that this Manner of difpofing of the Bow is in order to recover it with greater Quicknefs, but if in this Pofture it is aukward in Charging, it may be returned to the 1ft Pofition.

Come

4th, *Come to your cloſe Order.*

5th, *Port your Pike, and March.*

6th, *Charge.*

The three laſt Orders are only neceſſary, if, before the Bow is uſed, it is requiſite to charge with the Pike, which may happen on ſudden Occaſions.

If it is judged proper to charge Sword in hand, after uſing the Bow, which in the Attack of the Enemy in many Situations, when the Troops have to climb over interpoſing Objects, is the moſt rapid Manner of Aſſaulting, from the Weapon being uſed with one Hand; the Words of Order are:

1ſt, *Front Ranks return your Bows.*

2d,
Ground your Pikes. } This is always neceſſary in order not to be in the Way of the Ranks ruſhing forward.

3d, *Draw your Swords.*

4th, *Rear make ready, Preſent, Shoot, &c.*

In charging the Pike, the front **Rank** puſhes with it, held firm on the Hip, having about two

Feet

Feet in Referve, the fecond Rank pufhes with it overhanded above the other's Shoulder, the third Rank carries it ported; it would be utterly im- poffible for the Enemy's Bayonets to ftand the Charge, their Line would be overthrown with little Power of annoying their Adverfaries.

FOURTH

FOURTH POSITION.

The Archer Covered. Vide Fig. IV.

THE two former Pofitions are when the Archers act on the Offenfive. This, and the fubfequent Pofture, is when they act on the Defenfive,
if charged by Cavalry. The third Pofition is
ufed againft Infantry.

The Words of Order are :

ıft, { After planting their Pikes
Front Ranks, plant { they muft preferve the open
your Pikes. { Order.

2d, *Make ready, prefent.*

3d, *Shoot, &c.*

Nothing can be more formidable than this Pofture which Archers prefent to Cavalry ; from it
they act offenfive and defenfive at the fame Time.
The Enemy muft be fo occupied with the continual Difcharges of Arrows, that even if it were
poffible

poffible for them by any Means to beat down the Lances, yet the Attention of the Men and Horfes would be fo engaged from being in that Manner galled, that they could act with no Effect. It was from this Caufe, that in the ancient Battles, the Archers, though only fecured by a double Pallifade of Stakes, 6 to 8 Feet long, made on the Spur of Occafion by the Pioneers, could yet never be broke in upon by great Bodies of Men at Arms. But the Pike, with the Firmnefs given to it by the Spikes, prefents far more Security, and is an infinite Improvement. If the Horfe retreat, the Archers would continue their Attack, till they entirely routed them.

FIFTH

FIFTH POSITION.

The Archer couched. Vide Fig. V.

THIS is the second Defensive Posture, and is only used, when it may be judged necessary to strengthen the Stand of Pikes against Cavalry—and also at the near Distance to give an Opening to the Shot of the rear Rank.

The Words of Order are :

Front Rank fasten ⌠The Note in Page 48 is also ap-
your Bows.　⌡　plicable to this Motion.

Draw your Swords close to your Helms.

Charge at the Foot and couch low.

Middle and Rear, make ready, present.

Shoot, &c.

If the Enemy gives Way—then—

Front Rank, recover your Bows.

Make ready, present.

Shoot, &c.

It is fully sufficient for the front Rank alone to couch, in order to strengthen the Pikes, for if the front Line thereof is preserved, the second cannot be broke in upon.

SIXTH

SIXTH POSITION.

The Archer Marching.   Vide Fig. VI.

THIS is the laſt Poſture of the Archer, after Action, and preparatory to marching.

The Words of Order are :

Return your Bow.   { This is by putting it into the Sheath, on the Side of the Quiver, and paſſing them together to the right Shoulder.

Recover your Pike.
Shoulder your Pike.—March.

———————

This Manual Exerciſe is deſcribed as applying to the Complete Armed Archer, in order to give the Idea, how far he is capable of being fitted for Offence and Defence. But the Archers may be diſtinguiſhed into the Heavy and the Light Armed : the firſt having the complete Equipment; the latter

only

only the Sword and Bow, in order that they might act in various Situations, and in defultory Attack with the greater Rapidity and lefs Incumbrance, and then the Words of Order relative to the Pike are omitted.

As to the ufing the proof Helmet and Breaft Plate, or lighter Equipment, that is referred for Confideration, whether neceffary, when the Enemy does not ufe it, or as a Means of giving Confidence. The feveral Pofitions of the Archer are given as they appear the moft fimple, and naturally follow-ing each other defcriptive of his general Action; but it is neceffarily fuppofed that the Ufe of the Bow and Sword is previoufly learnt.* As to the various Evolutions attending the forming and act-ing in Line and Column, as they are nearly the fame with Archers as other Infantry, with the Dif-ference only of the Words of Order, thefe Ma-

* For Inftruction in learning the Ufe of the Bow, though requifite to be more fimplified, vide the fecond Book of Afcham's Toxophilus. The Manner of ufing the Sword cannot be better given, than by the Treatife on the Art of Defence on Foot with the Broad Sword and Sabre, pub-lifhed by Mr. Egerton.

nœuvres

nœuvres can be learnt from the fame Means.*
The Manual is the fame in Column as in the Line;
in changing the Difpofition in Action, the Archer
carries his Pike fhouldered, Bow ordered and
ported in the left Hand, and when formed, the
Words of Order are the two laft in the fecond
Pofition. When not in Action, all the Manœuvres are performed in the firft Pofition, with the
Bow returned. It is obvious that thefe Difpofitions
may be fo infinitely varied, as to exceed the Bounds
of the prefent Treatife to fpecify; the good Senfe
of thofe to whom it is addreffed, and the general

---

* The principal Manœuvres neceffary to the Archers are
1ft, The Open Column in Rear, Grenadiers; 2d, Open Column in Front, Light Infantry; 3d, Open Column on a
central Company; 4th, Change of Pofition in Column;
6th, Countermarch and Change of Pofition; 8th, March
in clofe Column; 11th, Change of Pofition; 12th, Retreat
in Line; 14th, the Hollow Square; 16th, Advancing in
Line, filing and charging to the Front; 17th, Retreating
in Line. Thefe Movements are felected from the Directions
for Evolutions of Infantry, to which the Numbers refer,
and may be learnt from the fame Means. The Variations
from the Words thereof, to open or clofe Column, refult
from the Neceffity of the Archers in Action or fecond Pofition preferving their open Order.

Knowledge

Knowledge of military Affairs, which at prefent pervades the Country, will foon point out the Mode of executing all that is neceffary. I fhall conclude therefore with fome general Obfervations on the Training the Archer for War, which appear of great Utility. The Ufe of the Bow is fo generally known, from the Number who practife for Amufement, (in feveral Counties it has never gone entirely to decay) and from the general Tendency in the People of this Country to Archery, that it is not neceffary to be very particular.

The Archer in training for War fhould accuftom himfelf to the ufing a Bow to the full of his Powers, without incommoding him; by Practice his Strength will increafe, and with it he fhould increafe the Force of his Bow; no one fhould fhoot in that of lefs Strength than requires 6olb. to draw the Arrow up, but as much ftronger as can be managed. The Shafts for Training, though blunt Piles, fhould be of equal Weight to the Sheaf Arrow, by which Means, though he does not practife with the latter, yet he will always know what it will do in Action, which

could

could not be the Cafe, if light Shafts were ufed.
He fhould alfo always exercife with the Quiver on
his left Side, in order to be expert in its Manage-
ment, and the handling and nocking the Shaft
in the fame Way, as when in the Line; accuf-
toming himfelf to long and ftrong Shooting, and to
obferve the Effect the Weather may have on his
Shaft. The Archer, in ftanding, fhould preferve
a free and erect Pofture; be fure in the Nocking
of his Shaft; and, in drawing, preferve the Height
of his Arm, according to the intended Elevation
of the Shaft, as pointed out in Fig. II. and IV.
bearing ftrongly with the Ball of the Hand, and
Force of the Bow-Arm, into the Handle, bringing the Strength of the whole Body as much as
poffible into Action with Steadinefs, Vigour,
and the greateft Celerity, loofing the Shaft in an
Inftant. The Aim is conducted by looking ftead-
faft at the Mark, not at the Shaft, and fuch is the
Direction given to the Limbs by the Eye, that
with the Information derived from knowing the
Nature of the Flight of his Shaft, the neceffary
Elevation will be foon habitually obtained. He
fhould

fhould beftow particular Attention to the judging of Diftance by roving; and in order to know when an Enemy comes within the Range of his Shot, I venture to fuggeft a Reflection which occurred to determine it, and prevent the Difplay of an Enemy's Line appearing nearer or farther off than in reality. When training, in fhooting at the Butt, the Archer fhould, with his Arm extended and Bow braced, compare the Height of Objects from Head to Foot, both of Horfe and Infantry at different Diftances, as they appear in Comparifon of the Altitude of the upper Part of the Bow, when looking over the Hand. By fettling the Memory of this in the Eye, or noting the general Marks of the Variations, he can always determine, with confiderable Precifion, the Diftance of the Enemy's Line. Of the Time that is neceffary, to form an Archer, it is obferved, that daily Practice for one Month, or three Times a Week for two Months, is adequate to make a fufficient Bowman for fhooting in Line.

F I N I S.